A BROKEN HEART IS AN ART

POROSH KHAN RANA

Printed in the United States of America

For any inquires or any feedback about this books
feel free contact to the writer
✉ poroshkhanrana05@gmail.com

A broken heart is an art

After recovering from a great illness
The doctor asked me the name of the medicine
What a strange do you see
I said your name

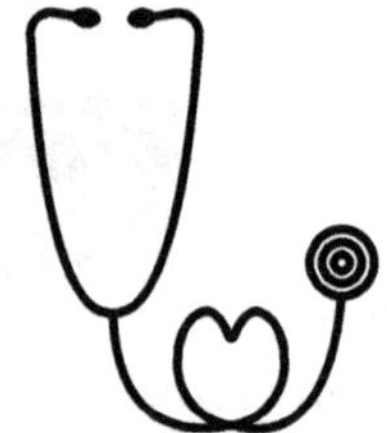

A broken heart is an art

Only at that moment, My eyes are filled
When You are in front of me
And the rest of the time I'm blind

A broken heart is an art

You can never forget me
Don't try that in vain
Have you ever seen the sun forgets the day
And the moon forgets the night?

A broken heart is an art

I wish trying to Touch You
But you are like the night
Where the sun is not able to reach

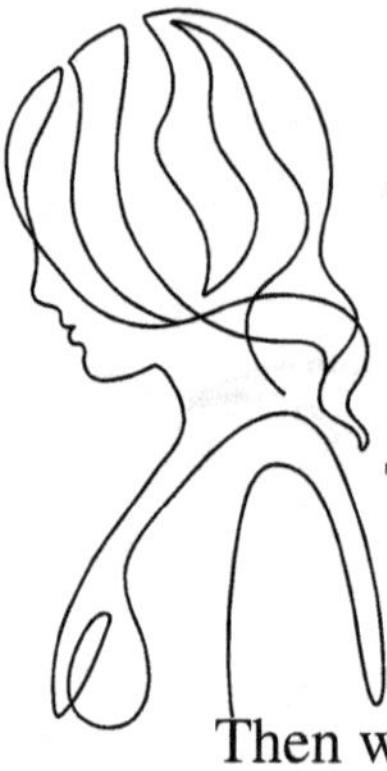

I am not the sky
That you can't touch me
I am not past time
That you can't bring me back
Nor am I not an alien
That you can't love me
Then what prevented you from being mine

A broken heart is an art

How will he understand your value?
Who got you without pursuit?
Near the hills where the clouds live
What is the value of the fog to its

I heard still some place for me in your heart
Please delete it now immediately
I also made this mistake one day
That's why I am passing this loss forever with tears in my eyes

A broken heart is an art

How much difference?
When she stays in front of my eyes
And when not stays
The Viewing eyes go asleep
But the eyes of the heart never sleep

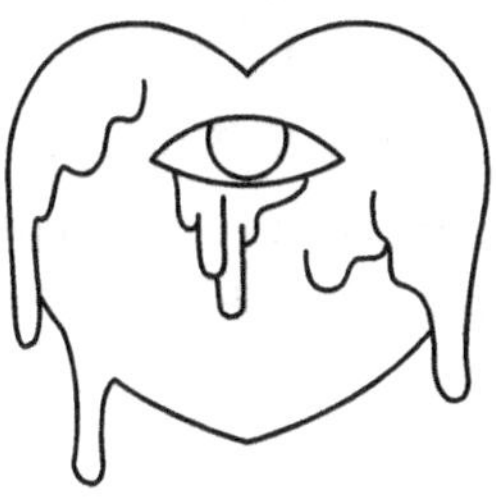

A broken heart is an art

Look she is how great?
Whose I asked for little happiness,
But she didn't give it
Again without asking gave me a sea of sorrow

A broken heart is an art

What you say in your mouth is a lie
What you say in your eyes is true
We see only deep thirst in the desert
But the history of the ocean is also hidden in its chest

A broken heart is an art

I heard that time takes away everything
But this is not completely true
Time took you away from me
But your memories still couldn't take away

A broken heart is an art

Dress yourself up a bit
If not for myself but for me
You can be worthless to everyone else in the world
But you are a great medicine for my eyes

A broken heart is an art

I heard that
People don't understand the value of everything
When they get it easily
So wine is worth more than knowledge here

A broken heart is an art

Oh my heart, fear not your love was not wrong
For that she punished you
People kill the peacocks
just for his beautiful feathers

A broken heart is an art

Easy to forget
But we don't want to forget
So we say all our life
forgetting is a hard work

A broken heart is an art

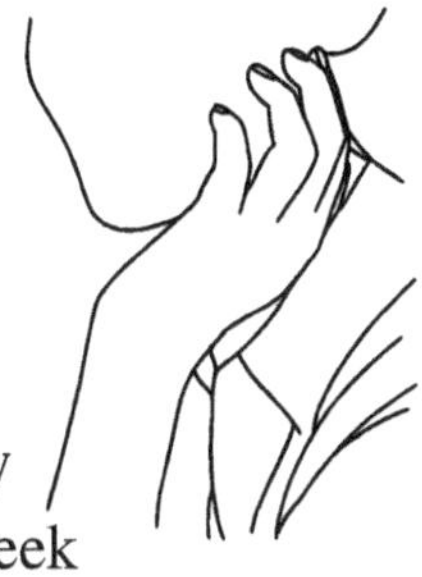

I was very sick
Then came doctor
When each doctor failed and went away
Then she came and laughed at her rose cheek
The result was she healed me and went away

A broken heart is an art

As it may be I am different today from previous,
But look at my heart
There was never a change at any time.

A broken heart is an art

How do you think?
That the distance will take you away from me?
You are like that kite
As high as it rises
The thread of kite reels will be just as strong

A broken heart is an art

How do you believe?
I forgot.
Does it ever rain without clouds?

A broken heart is an art

When I remember you
I become cheerful
Have you thought about it once
How do I live with the sacrifice of this happiness

A broken heart is an art

Never get him again
Who wanted to have you, not your body.
Thousands of people will find
who wants to get your body not you.

A broken heart is an art

Since that day I have been blinded
That day I met my dearest
But she didn't look at me
I will never get my eyesight back again
Unless she looks at me when we meet again

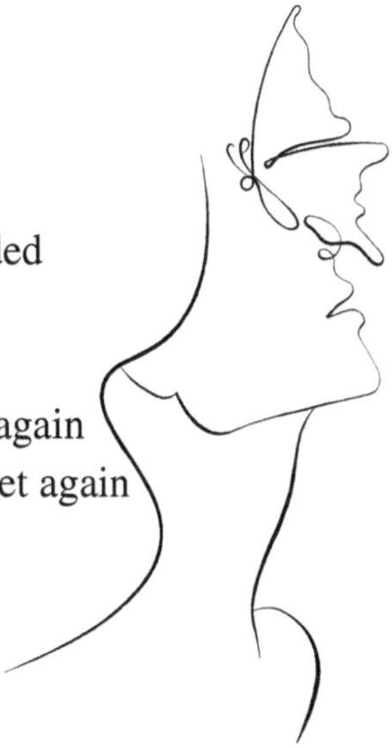

A broken heart is an art

The one I wanted to forget
My mind remembered her more
And whom I wanted to remember
My mind had forgotten her

A broken heart is an art

No matter how many stormy in your life
Never feel alone in the world
Look, the moon rises alone in the sky
But millions of stars arise to take care of the moon

A broken heart is an art

She is none of mine
But she is my heartbeat
So keep my heart beating
I love her

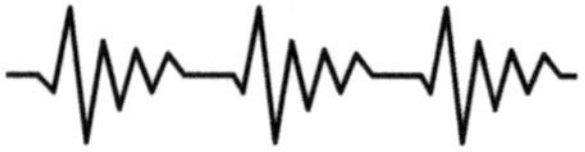

A broken heart is an art

As much as you you want to push me away
I will be closer to your heart
Look at night
As much as it wants to hide in dark
It closer gets to dawn

A broken heart is an art

Even my worst enemy praised me
Whenever I did him a favor for the first time in my life
And my best friend too
Condemned me for only one mistake
Whom I have helped all my life

A broken heart is an art

As much as I was punished for love
I didn't get it for the biggest crime of my life

A broken heart is an art

When I didn't love her
She started loving me
Whenever I started loving her
Since then she started hating me

A broken heart is an art

As much as I want to get closer to her
She passed me like a shadow
Again whenever I want to come back from her
She follows me in the same shadow
So now, what else can I do without loving her?

When I started hating everyone
Then everyone started loving me
Again whenever I started loving everyone
Then everyone started hating me

A broken heart is an art

I can't hold you captive in my love
The ground can too never touch the clouds
Until the clouds come down as rain

A broken heart is an art

Who can't stand me today
She had a smile on her face
And I was the reason

A broken heart is an art

Ever since I wanted to be free
From the sorrow given by my dearest
I've been dying of lack of happiness ever since

A broken heart is an art

Have you ever desired to love me?
One day the sea dries up and becomes a desert
Are you never wanted to come back to me?
Even the distant clouds return to the sea one day

A broken heart is an art

You can't forget me
As people can never forget their own name
You won't even get me
For example, there are no colors in the rainbow

A broken heart is an art

Today One more time arrange the flower garden
Maybe she will come
Or will not come
My only benefit is that time
Which that time I will wait for her

A broken heart is an art

Take me once
To my beloved
I will bring back my heart
If she doesn't give back
I will bring her

A broken heart is an art

Do you think I forget you?
For if you fall in front of me I don't look
I'm just acting but you'll never understand

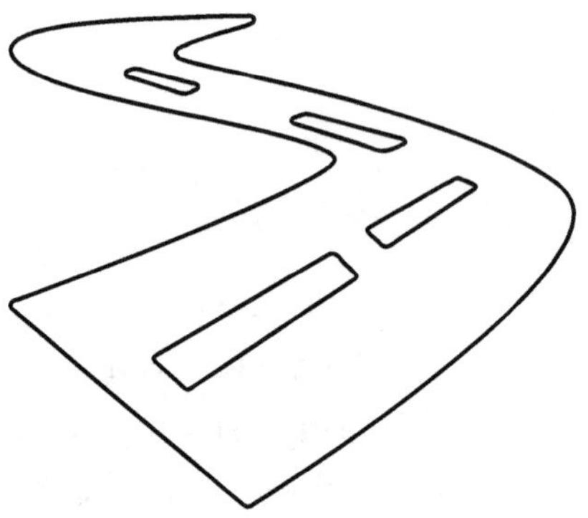

A broken heart is an art

I knowingly
I have deposited my heart to the betrayer
So I don't know whose to blame now
Her? or me?

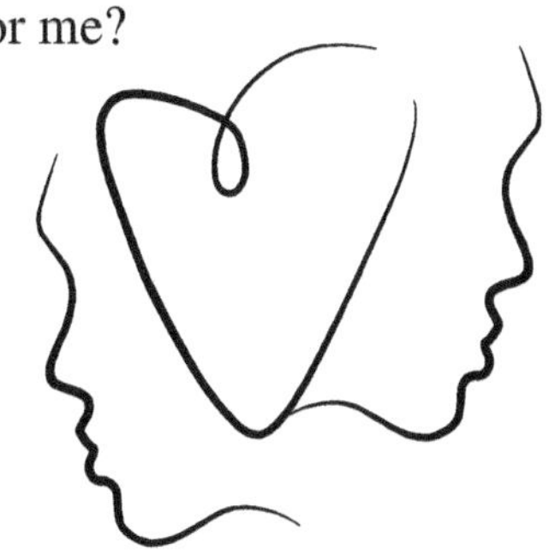

A broken heart is an art

Tear to shreds my heart
Then cast out that magician
Who has taken my heart without being within me

A broken heart is an art

I don't have anything else to say on your birthday except to wish you
Because for whose one you were born for
You are not his

A broken heart is an art

If I want I can forget you
But I don't want to forget you
You are such a pain in my heart
Even feelings of happiness never give me this

A broken heart is an art

I have never wanted so much happiness
She gave me everything without asking
Then when I get used to happiness
Since then she has been giving me grief

A broken heart is an art

I tried to convince her many times
Who never wanted to understand
I told the sea about the drought
Which its never supposed to understand

A broken heart is an art

The brightness that enters my heart
Once I see you
No one ever can't walk the path of that brightness
and end that path

A broken heart is an art

Happiness is an expensive market commodity
And I am a cheap market buyer
Have you ever heard of it?
Expensive market products are sold in the cheap market

A broken heart is an art

I could easily forget you
If my heart were like eyes
My eyes can be good without seeing you
But my heart can't do it even for a moment

A broken heart is an art

As deep as you can dive into the water
You can climb just as high
Step back as far as you can in preparation for the jump
Your jump distance will increase accordingly

A broken heart is an art

Don't look for love by word of mouth
Love is like the ocean
Over which huge waves stormed
But deep down there is a kingdom of silence

A broken heart is an art

Those Who told you I love you
None of them didn't remember you today
But that said I hate you so much
Look and see that he is the only one who still remembers you

A broken heart is an art

Everyone will forget you only except one
The one who told you I hate you

A broken heart is an art

Before I loved her,
I didn't know what is sadness
She gave me her love
And taught me what is sadness

A broken heart is an art

She didn't leave me
Or I didn't leave her either
Only fate left us
So we never get together

A broken heart is an art

I am grateful to her
Whose love I had become worthless
I am really grateful to her
Because her separation turned me from stone to gold

A broken heart is an art

I will never blame her
For she is not mine
I will blame myself the whole life
Because I wanted her even though fate was not written

A broken heart is an art

From now on, no one can't ever imprison me
Even for the crime of Hiroshima or Nagasaki
When she looked at me
And captured my heart

A broken heart is an art

When she describes my faults
I have no way except for being dumb at that moment
Because if I open my mouth
She will turn from an angel to a devil

Tell him what to say other than crazy
He knows the wait will never end but he waits

A broken heart is an art

How do you think that?
Now no more love between us?
Air can also touch the body
But what can touch the heart?

A broken heart is an art

Heart began to love her
Who broke him into pieces
And began to break her
Who came to build him

A broken heart is an art

Oh, my heart?
Why die of happiness when you see her
Can dead people ever be cheerful?
Seeing his own killer

My mistake was that
I locked myself in a cage without asking
Consciousness return then,
When I saw that no one want to hunt captive birds

A broken heart is an art

One day she will realize that,
I only loved her the most in the world
But will anyone ever go hunting captive birds?
Where thousands of free birds roam the forest

Whether the sword is sharp or rusty
She will win this battle
Where the smile on her face is the biggest weapon
There I will forever be defeated by her

What am I capable of? to get you by logic?
Where I didn't get you by love
But look what a big player you
You bought me only by hate

A broken heart is an art

If you want mind satisfaction
Please hide your good deeds as much as possible
And reveal your bad deeds to the peoples

A broken heart is an art

I don't want to look at you
Just because of this fear
If I love again

A broken heart is an art

If my sins were reflected in the mirror
Then first of all in this world, I would have been hanged

A broken heart is an art

Who will buy me as a slave?
I sold out a long time ago
In exchange for her smile

A broken heart is an art

Everyone can laugh
But how many can do it like her?
Many people can hurt
But how many can give happiness passed through the pain?

A broken heart is an art

The very big arrogant heart her
So she does not understand the cry of my clay heart
Consciousness will return by then her
When she knows arrogance will be mixed with soil

A broken heart is an art

What prevented you from smiling at seeing me?
You know
I have never wanted anything from you but except for this

A broken heart is an art

Your Heart Also Made of Clay?
I really want to know
Or else why so much difference with my heart?

A broken heart is an art

Everyone was leaving one by one
I didn't think you also would be like them
But when it happened
I realized I was wrong to know

A broken heart is an art

Was it my fault alone?
That I had to bear everything?
Even if no one else knew, she knew exactly

A broken heart is an art

Why do you want to get the one who you lost?
Oh, broken heart of mine?
Purpose of the destination once the train leaves the platform
Does it come back again?

A broken heart is an art

I heard that the ocean can float everything
Even also a whole city
I dived into deep
then why couldn't the ocean drown my sorrow

A broken heart is an art

Do not go to judge the deceivers
She will cheat again
And you will also face it again

A broken heart is an art

I could also wait
If I was assured even for one time
This wait will end one day

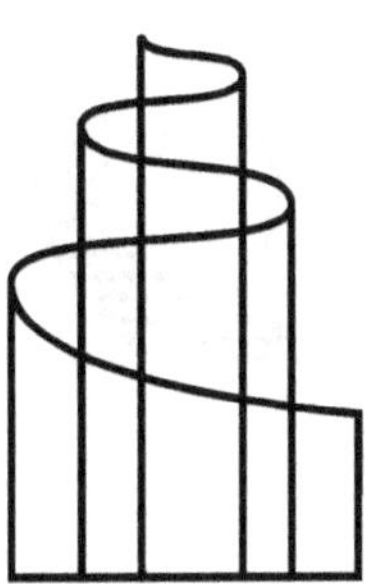

A broken heart is an art

Many people will come along the way in life
Only they will remain
Those will reach the path of the heart

When I met you suddenly
I didn't realize you would talk to me
But I knew that
Sometimes impossible things happen in this world

I was waiting
That too for almost an era
However, You come but didn't ask me
How are you?

A broken heart is an art

For that, we all wait for a long time
That's the unpleasant waiting is death

www.ingramcontent.com/pod-product-compliance
Lightning Source LLC
LaVergne TN
LVHW052052160826
845678LV00015B/3180

* 9 7 9 8 3 7 0 9 2 6 6 5 5 *